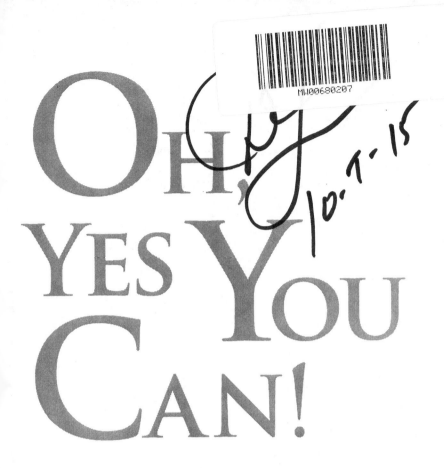

OH, YES YOU CAN!

A HOW TO GUIDE FOR REBUILDING CONFIDENCE AND ACHIEVING SUCCESS

DELORES PRESSLEY
SUE MACKEY

Dimensions Plus Publishing
P. O. Box 9049
Canton, OH 44711
Phone 330.669.9809

Copyright ©2010 by DeLores Pressley Worldwide LLC & The Mackey Group LLC

Printed in the United States of America

ISBN-13:   978-0-9726172-4-6

ISBN-10:   0-9726172-4-8

Table of Contents

Introduction

Have you ever left a self-help seminar feeling more inspired than you ever have before to remedy all that has gone awry in your life? You're motivated to do whatever it takes. You're ready to change your life and become the biggest success story ever told. You've got it all figured out… at least for a day or two… then you lose that momentum as quickly as you found it, and life goes on as it did. Sound familiar?

There are a plethora of self-help books and memoirs that have been written over the last fifty years, all with the intent of educating and informing people who value success. There are also untold numbers of speakers (many of them highly skilled) explaining what we need to do to succeed. While the books, speakers, DVDs and CDs tell us what to do, the overwhelming majority of us are still searching for *how* to do it. You know — the real substance.

So what makes this book different? We talk about how to rebuild your confidence — the confidence you had in your earliest years of life, the confidence that is essential to success. *Oh, Yes You Can!* will help you understand not only what to do to achieve your goals, but how to do it and do it well. We are passionate about you knowing these things and achieving your dreams. *Oh, Yes You Can!* focuses on the how, what and why.

The difference between what and how is the reason most of us who aspire to success never reach our self-defined, desired success level. It's true that it takes more than learning what to do. But we fail to get that because no one is teaching us the *how* part of the equation. For people who read or hear *what* to do and think, "Yeah, it's easy for you, but not for me," the *how* is very important. Or perhaps you're among those who always want to ask those you see as more successful, "How did you *really* do it?" If any of this sounds familiar, you're not alone, and this book is for you.

Think about it. We hear and learn that we must fake it until we make it — just do it! And sometimes we are told that if we act confident, confidence will come. There's nothing wrong with any of those statements if one knows the "how" behind them. If we don't know *how* to "just do it" though, failure is a given. Learning how is the key to success.

We've been told that practice makes perfect and that if you want to master something, you should practice it over and over again. Practicing the same thing over and over does not lead to perfection, nor does it lead to mastery. It only causes more failure if you don't know how to practice using the right skill sets. When we routinely practice using the wrong skills, it stands to reason the outcome will be mastered or perfected failure.

Imagine telling someone who is trying to hit a baseball to just keep swinging the bat. She swings, but keeps missing the ball and can't make the connection. Telling her to keep practicing the same failed skills she's been using will only make her a master at missing the ball. She knows what to do as a batter — stand at home plate with the bat ready to hit the ball when the pitcher throws the pitch. But no one has taught her how to be a hitter. She does not know or use the skills required to be a good hitter. Practicing all day long won't help her unless she knows how to skillfully hit balls.

What does practicing the wrong skills do to our psyche? We eventually tell ourselves we can't do it. We're right. Simply put, we can't do it if we keep using the wrong skills or don't know how to use the right skills. It's what happens to so many people trying to succeed with only the knowledge of what to do and no knowledge of how to do it or how to do it well — the skill sets needed for success.

In this book, *Oh, Yes You Can!*, you will learn what to do to gain confidence and how to go about it. Our commitment to you is that you'll read this book and learn why you've tried to act confident, yet find sustainable confidence has eluded you.

You'll learn how to make the success tips you've learned and despaired of start to work for you. We know you can, and you will know it by the time you finish reading *Oh, Yes You Can!*

Keep this in mind as you read: you possess the power to change. You also possess the power to be a confident and significant person. The key is in knowing *how* to hone in on the right skills and put them to work for you.

We are rooting for your success!

C H A P T E R   O N E

In the Beginning

Visualize a newborn. All babies are born with brains that are virtually empty. Now think of our brains as computers. Our brains at birth are like computers with no software loaded and no programs to work from. The brain's receptors, like the hard drive, are functioning but cannot work until loaded with software. Like computers, we become what we load in. And also like computers, we *can* delete what we've put into the hard drive. It takes a series of steps to do that, though.

Our earliest years are spent loading our brains with input from our environment, our parents, family members, caregivers, friends and teachers. Whether it's learning to eat meals with utensils, becoming potty trained, learning to walk and talk, dressing, learning to read and write or riding a bike, each task we learned and mastered was met with great enthusiasm and bragging rights.

For those who influenced us in our early years, enthusiasm about everything we learned to do was a result of their faith in us. They knew we could do it. They had confidence in us. And that enthusiasm reinforced our confidence, which caused us to keep practicing until we mastered the task. We were encouraged to try new things and did so with reckless abandon. Our brains began to identify learning, repetition and practice until we perfected the task to get praise. To keep trying until we mastered each new skill was a given. We didn't even know the word "failure" existed. Falling off our bikes was no reason to give up. It was a reason to try again, learn new skills and practice them. We were encouraged, taught how, and assisted until we mastered the task.

> *"I have not failed. I've just found 10,000 ways that won't work."*
> – Thomas Edison

But then real life intruded. As we got older, developed more skills, mastered simple and complex tasks, life began to change. Expectations were still high from those who influenced us. Our brains were loaded with those expectations and, at times, confidence beyond our abilities and skills. Those around us always gave us the benefit of the doubt that we could master age-level tasks – we were smart, they said. We'd demonstrated it a bunch of times.

Our brains grew accustomed to expecting praise. If we couldn't get it right the first, second or third time, it was not a problem. "Just keep practicing," they told us, and the praise came with or without failure but always with encouragement to practice more. Mastery was the big prize, a guarantee of exceptional praise. It was heaped on us when we finally "got it."

By second and third grade, the high expectations and praise suddenly came with conditions attached. We were confused because we didn't know how to process these new conditions. There were new rules imposed for when and how to achieve success in learning and mastering new skills, tasks and concepts. No one explained why there were new rules; we just know things were different. We soon found that praise was harder to come by, criticism more consistent. There were so many new experiences bombarding us every day, many of which were totally foreign, and we were expected to know how to process information and master tasks on the first or second try. Slowly, our heightened confidence level began to diminish.

And too, as if by magic, we now were expected to be on our way to perfection. We were supposed to master all things with the greatest of ease. This was especially true for young girls. The expectation was to learn faster than boys, always do the right thing and know what that right thing was. Boys, on the other hand, will be boys, and got away with just being boys. There were expectations for boys, but if they underperformed and didn't meet them, it was not a big deal, because they were boys. But for girls, not meeting expectations was considered a flaw.

For some of us, being mother's little helper was a status worth attaining and, at times, a curse. A curse because expectations were that we knew what to do in that role and could perform it flawlessly. Be the perfect little helper. We had no road map and no life experiences to prepare us for this role, as we'd soon discover. Our brains were being taken over by mixed messages.

Upon receiving the esteemed title of "mother's little helper" or "little man of the house," our confidence soared but only momentarily. We were now the administrative assistant to the household's leader, the chief executive officer. Administrative assistants wield power—it's no entry-level position. We had just learned to tie our shoes, ride a bike, say our ABCs, spell our name and dress ourselves. Not well, but we did it, and now we were catapulted up the ladder of authority.

Our life experiences were few. Those we did have, for good or bad, weren't processed from an adult mind, but from a child's mind with few skills or resources to make sense of it all. But with our new title came the confidence that we were on our way to bigger and better things. That was until we began to get negative feedback on our performance. Expectations were high, but performance was found to be lacking. We soon discovered being an administrative assistant wasn't all it was cracked up to be.

This, too, was absorbed into our brains. Still needing and wanting praise and acceptance, the kind we received and grew to anticipate as toddlers, we began striving for per-fection. Our confidence, instead of building, started to diminish, replaced by doubt and hoop-jumping. It was as if someone had completely deleted our excellent software and replaced it with far inferior stuff. Succeeding now was a struggle at every turn.

We didn't like it, didn't have the skill sets yet to process it, but since it's all we had, criticism filled our brains, replacing our once bullet-proof confidence with doubts and fears. Failures were no longer met with encouragement from adults or even from other kids. But what could we do? Our minds were fertile receptors to all input, good and bad. We absorbed the criticism from others and self-doubt grew even bigger.

> *"How often in life we complete a task that was beyond the capability of the person we were when we started it."*
> – John Powell

So after struggling, trying to get it right, to receive acceptance, some of us resorted to people-pleasing. We'd do anything to have others accept, praise or like us. Pleasing people became our full-time job. It required us to strive for perfection. Not our concept of perfection, but everyone else's, and no two are the same.

It was an impossible task, and we lost ourselves trying to accomplish it. Our identity and our inherent talents became clouded with the need to please others. The cost was high, but what did we know? We were clueless that people-pleasing and confidence are opposite of each other. Our world became a daily experience of doubts, fears and longing for acceptance.

While some of us became people-pleasers, others just gave up trying. They had tried pleasing, and it didn't work. They figured, "What's the use? Nothing I do is right, so I may as well do whatever I please. The results will be the same anyway, if criticism is all there is." It may appear this behavior was a search for self-confidence, and in part it was, but it was also a search for attention, acceptance and praise from anyone, even for bad behavior.

The point is, we load our brains with negative or positive input, and we react. Most of that input is loaded into our brains by our environment and life experiences. The majority of the time, we are unaware of the upload; it's not a conscious effort. If we hear enough bad stuff about ourselves, hear enough criticism, it fills up space in our heads. It gets stuck in there. It needs space, so it pushes the good stuff out of the way. Over time the negative completely takes over, always searching for more space to store the input and replace our self-confidence.

In order to retrieve our confidence, the confidence we had so much of as toddlers, we have to be very selective about what goes into our minds. What goes in will come out in attitude, thoughts and actions.

You've proven many times that you are capable. Keep reading, and you'll discover not only *what* to do but *how* to do it.

> *Oh, Yes You Can! Tip: Retrieve those confidence-building affirmations you heard as a young child. It is possible to reprogram your brain and rebuild your confidence! Replace the space occupied by not being good enough and not being perfect enough with more positive, confidence-building thoughts and experiences. We promise, you'll recapture that feeling of Oh, Yes I Can!*

Before we move to the next chapter, you should beware of a common enemy. It's not a person but a misunderstood and misused word: "perfect." Trying to be perfect is an impossible goal. And it's just plain craziness in the making! It saps our confidence and buries those gifts and talents we were born with. There is no such thing as absolute perfection. Perfection, like success, is defined differently by everyone.

If you aren't convinced, listen to two women and their ideas of a perfectly clean house. One is completely obsessed about cleaning. She cleans floor to ceiling, under and over everything, weekly. By the time she's through, dust is already accumulating. The other woman does half the work and claims her house has been perfectly cleaned, too. Who has attained perfection? Neither has. It's an illusion and a concept held by the individual. If confidence is tied to perfection as an absolute, it will never be attainable. Don't hold yourself up to a standard that is beyond your ability as a human.

Our message is a simple one. In order to build confidence, we must start at the beginning, dumping the negative doubts and fears from the space they occupy in our minds. We must surround ourselves with influences that will enable us to be confident. It won't be as hard as you think, and we'll help you along the way.

C H A P T E R T W O

Boosters and Robbers

With our youth behind us, we move into adulthood. But the impact of our life experiences, good or bad, remains with us. It has become the framework for our belief system and values, and for our expectations of ourselves and others. Our confidence or lack of it, resulting from our life experiences up to this point, will largely determine what we choose to do with our lives, the people we choose to surround ourselves with, and, ultimately, our well-being.

> *"Keep away from people who try to belittle your ambitions. Small people always do that, but the really great make you feel that you, too, can become great."*
> – Mark Twain

Some experts tell us that the past has no value. In reality, it does have value and can't be tossed aside. Our past is a vital part of who we are. Our life experiences do set a foundation for our belief systems and values. And for those of us who have had the misfortune of abysmal childhoods, loss, traumatic events or just lousy circumstances, understanding our past allows us to understand and reframe our present.

The past is important. Understanding our past, not to blame or condemn, has value for who we can become. What we can learn from it holds treasures that will serve us and help others to have a better present and future life. We all know people who have found just one treasure hidden in the wreckage of a difficult childhood, who took that one piece of good fortune and used it to regain their confidence, excel in their chosen work, and find personal happiness.

> ***Oh, Yes You Can! Tip:*** *Explore your past searching for the nuggets of goodness inside any wreckage. When you understand where you came from (and the value of both negative and positive circumstances and events), you'll see more clearly what's holding you back now. Take stock of the changes you need to focus on to move forward, and use the good stuff to your advantage!*

Exploring our past, searching for the nuggets of goodness, we'll find that we are well equipped to launch a rebuilding of our confidence. The search will reveal a lot about our skills, ability and knowledge. Not just academic knowledge, but our life experiences — joys and sorrows, successes and failures — will be the foundation for rebuilding our faith in ourselves.

Also take note of the negative or bad things in your childhood. They happen, whether on account of someone else's actions or because of events beyond anyone's control. The good news is, we learned coping skills to get through it all, even if those skills were self-taught. We also experienced the many faces of humanity and learned to deal with real life and adversities early on. Some of those skill sets we acquired have served us well and will continue to serve us throughout our lives, providing greater faith in ourselves. What we'll learn as we go forward is how to make those old skills work for us and not undermine us as we strive to rebuild our confidence.

Most important right now is to understand how to jump start the rebuilding process. Confidence cannot be attained without a support system. We can't sustain confidence all by our lonesome. That is a ridiculous notion.

When we explore the past, we find two types of people: confidence boosters and confidence robbers. The confidence boosters were those who cheered us on and boosted our confidence every step of the way. The confidence robbers were those who tried or succeeded in beating down or stealing our confidence. They robbed us by incessant criticism, criticism without solutions or caring guidance, abusive or bad behaviors, unrealistic expectations, bullying, and the list goes on.

With both types of people, looking back will help us move forward. Yes, even the robbers are helpful in this respect. How? They fit a profile, and we want to remember what that profile looks like and the damage they can cause. Forgetting, we could end up befriending, marrying, living with, or working for these people. Or we could turn out to be like them. We want none of the above.

In our youth we had few choices or, if we could choose, we didn't have enough life experience or skill sets behind us to make better choices. In our adult life, it's different. Don't forget who these people are and their character traits. They are not the folks we want in our support system. We want to be deliberate and selective with our confidence-building support network. That's one of the benefits of the past. We know who we want and need around us, and we know who we don't need. We've experienced both, and now we get to choose.

> ***Oh, Yes You Can! Tip:*** *Seek out and surround yourself with confidence boosters. Those who make you feel good about being you!*

Who do we need and want in our support network? Think of at least one person, or more, who believed in you and your ability to accomplish a new task or encouraged you to do something you'd never done before. This person could have been a parent, teacher, sibling, relative or even a stranger. They may have offered just a kind word or a good piece of advice; better yet, this person may have helped you each step of the way, like a guide through the woods. You may not have appreciated it at the time, but you remembered it later.

You may recall your early youth when everything you accomplished or learned became a heroic event in the family. You may have been loved and supported by a particular family member, teacher or friend. Someone who, when you were in his or her presence, made you feel really good, valued and appreciated. This person believed in you whether you did or not. He or she may have expected more from you than you expected from yourself but showed you how you could achieve it and kept encouraging you to press on.

Search the past for evidence. Make a list of one or more people who had confidence in you just because you were you. Recall the good feelings, the memories of what it felt like. If you grew weak, they encouraged you to press on. When you succeeded, they offered praise and raised the bar, knowing you could master the next task. It is important to remember these people from your past, because you want to recall that feeling of confidence and support. You will feel it again as you rebuild.

Another reason you need to look back and explore, is that we're going to ask you to begin a search for a feel-good person — a confidence booster — who you can be around, if you don't already have one in your life today.

We can't rebuild and sustain confidence without at least one person believing in us. Relationships do matter. It matters who we choose to be around, and it matters who we connect with. The questions we must ask are: When I'm around this person, is it a positive or negative experience? Does it contribute to my well-being, emotionally and mentally, or does it rob me of my self-worth, my confidence and my significance in this world?

Let's begin rebuilding our confidence by replacing the confidence robbers and their input in our minds and hearts with the good stuff from confidence boosters and their input. This will help us start to experience the thrill and power of having confidence and significance again.

C H A P T E R   T H R E E

Self-Sabotage

*"Stop overestimating the power of others while under-
estimating your own. The minute you stop caring
about what others say, think or do, their power
vanishes — giving you the power to find your own."*
– DeLores Pressley

In the previous chapter, you were asked to identify a person
who is on your side — a confidence booster: a person who
believes in, encourages and supports you, regardless of your
imperfections. You may have identified more than one; if so,
all the better. Whomever you've identified, that person will
play an important role in rebuilding your faith in yourself.
Before you attempt to access this person's needed support,
let's first determine if you are sabotaging yourself. If so, we
need to change those dynamics.

*"Whether you think you can or you think you can't –
you are right."*
– Henry Ford

Many of us have read or heard that to gain confidence all we have to do is think it, and we will have it. It's true that if we believe we can't, we can't. And if we believe we can, we can. It does take a little more than just thinking it and believing it though. Thinking and believing without the right action will end in defeat.

Rebuilding confidence, gaining confidence in anything, is a process, not a one-time event. It requires some skills. If we skip the process of acquiring lasting confidence and depend solely on one successful event, chances are we'll lose the confidence again, and quickly.

The process begins with discovering the origins of our lack of confidence. When and how did it happen? If we know the cause, we can treat the symptoms much faster and more effectively.

For example, if we were raised with constant criticism and nothing we did was ever good enough, we'll work overtime on criticism avoidance. We won't risk getting criticized. Doing nothing, staying in the shadows, feels easier on us. We may avoid making new friends and trying new things, or avoid uncomfortable situations. In the end, we've allowed others to be confidence robbers by their words and behaviors. Then, without knowing what we're doing, we pick up where they left off.

Oh, Yes You Can! Tip: Don't be your own confidence robber! By finding fault and criticizing ourselves, we shut out joy and life's many rewards. It's not healthy and can be very damaging to the spirit. Look for the good in you! Feel confident that you are worthy of praise from yourself and others.

Let's see if we can identify the cause of our lack of confidence. Can you identify or relate with any of the reasons listed below?

1. You're trying to attain perfection.
2. You're highly critical of yourself and others.
3. You've made some bad mistakes, poor choices.
4. You've failed and beat yourself up.
5. You think you're not good enough and don't deserve it.
6. People in your present and past criticized and judged you.
7. You've been out of the loop for too long and feel inadequate.
8. You compare yourself to others.
9. You just feel empty, unmotivated — a pain that won't go away.
10. You must be able to do it well before you try just doing it.

11. You're unable to find humor in life and feel susceptible to the human condition.
12. You're unable to manage your emotions and relationships well.

You've probably found a reason or two, maybe more, from this list for your lack of confidence. Or maybe you've added one or two to the list. Here's the good news! Any and all of these causes are fixable. It won't be hard, and we're here to show you how. And don't forget your confidence booster will be on your side, too.

Oh, Yes You Can! Action: Promise yourself that from this point forward you will not allow anyone, yourself or others, to rob you of your confidence. Talk yourself through the moment when those negativities surface. Refuse to complete the thought. Counter it with something positive that was said to you or about you. You're human; these thoughts will surface if it's all you've known. Try to catch them, stop them and fill that space with something good.

Let's look deeper at each of the twelve possible causes for little or no confidence on the list above. Let's see what we can do to convince you that none of them deserve all the energy given to them; they have no value and, as you'll see, are highly destructive. (You will learn the skills you need to eliminate this negativity from your life in another chapter).

1. *You're trying to attain perfection.* There is no such thing as a perfect human being. It's pure nonsense. Besides, each person's idea of perfect is subjective, through their eyes only and determined by what? We'll never know. Being of good character and having a good and willing attitude — not perfect, but striving to be a better human being — is what we want to achieve.

2. *You're highly critical of yourself and others.* This confidence drain is tied to perfection, and there's no such thing. This is one of those cases of "lighten up" on yourself and others. So much self-criticism and criticism of others isn't really important. Start questioning if your criticism really has value to you or to others. Most does not. Some of it will. Begin to eliminate that which is not important. Stop yourself when you start to get critical.

3. *You've made some bad mistakes, poor choices.* Welcome to real life. Anyone who has not made bad mistakes or poor choices is not living life as it was intended. Don't stay stuck on it. Learn from it. What went wrong and why, are good questions. What can you do to make amends if others were affected? What can you do to prevent the same from happening again? Forgive yourself, forgive others and ask

for forgiveness; then get on with your life and all that you have learned from the experience. Add it to your list of "don't do that again."

4. *You've failed and beat yourself up.* Again, welcome to the real world of being human. Failure is a human condition. Learn from it and do what is necessary to clean up any wreckage you can, then move on. Failure is part of life because no one has all the answers. Ask for help from those who have been where you want to go; if you fail to do that, you'll remain stuck. Your confidence will come from the learning experience. You become an expert in what not to do in a similar situation.

5. *You think you're not good enough and don't deserve it.* What a crock! Someone put that in your head and you need to push it right on out. We have each been born with skills and talents. As a human being, you are equal to all others regardless of where you came from. You deserve a good life, and how you define "good" is totally up to you. If you want to compete in athletics and don't have coordination and talent, move on to something else. Focus on areas in which you do have talent and skills. If you don't know what those areas are, try things that interest you, and you'll find them. Ask others what they have observed about you and get their input. Don't beat yourself up or let others lead you down a road you don't want to travel.

6. *People in your past and present judge and criticize you.* Follow that old maxim of "know thyself." If it's constructive criticism, meant to help you succeed in life, then listen and act upon it. If, like most criticism, it's not constructive, let the person know that you no longer allow confidence-robbing in your life. Explain the negative effect of their words on you, and also be prepared to explain what will help you.

7. *You've been out of the loop for too long and feel inadequate.* You have lots of company, and there are many stories told about how people found their passion in life after years of being out of the loop. Confidence will come with action. Find something of interest to you and be willing to start where you must to acquire the skills and knowledge that will enable you to move forward from that point. Many people have jumped-started their career late in life and flourished. You must take action, and that will lead to other opportunities.

8. *You compare yourself to others.* Stop! You are not someone else and never could be. Chances are if you knew these people behind closed doors, you'd choose to remain you. You have no idea what burdens they have now, burdens they've had in the past or what will happen in their futures. You've got you and you know you, warts and all. Be the best version of you — with your skills, talents, abilities, and yes, looks. Improve upon you and let go trying to be someone else. If you admire character traits of another person — for

instance, if someone is kind and considerate, then work at being kinder and more considerate, too. That you can do.

9. *You just feel empty, unmotivated — a pain that won't go away.* First, make sure nothing is physically wrong and that you don't have a chemical or hormonal imbalance. If you're healthy, start listening to your self-talk. Pay attention to it. This is important. You'll learn what you're rehashing over and over, unconsciously. If it's negative and hurtful stuff, it may be causing you to feel this way. Also consider whether any of the following could be causing this feeling of emptiness: food allergies, lack of exercise, not enough sleep, being overwhelmed, or a loss or recent adversity. Some of what we cover in later chapters may be of great help to you. Read on. Start paying attention to you, your thoughts and actions, to find a pattern.

10. *You must be able to do it well before you try just doing it.* Don't get stuck in the need to be perfect. We rarely, if ever, try something new and are able to do it perfectly from the start. If you're worried about what others may think of you, stop that, too. Wonder what they'd think of you for not trying because you're afraid? Now that's worth thinking about, not what they'll think if you don't do it well.

11. *You're unable to find humor in being human and feel susceptible to the human condition.* Taking oneself too seriously is not healthy. In fact, it can be very depressing. Laughing at oneself

and all that transpires around us everyday is good for the soul. If nothing else, it may extend your life. Laughing cures a lot of our problems.

12. *You're unable to manage your emotions and relationships well.* This is a common challenge for many people. We will cover this in detail later in the book, identifying the skills you need and why you need them to develop sustaining and rewarding relationships. Managing emotions is a critical aspect of relationships. Both require numerous skill sets. You have many of them but knowing how to use them more effectively is the key.

> *"We probably wouldn't worry about what people think of us if we could know how seldom they do."*
> – Olin Miller

CHAPTER   FOUR

Gold Nuggets

By now you have identified the confidence boosters, who supported and rooted for you at some time in your life. You've also identified probable causes of your low self-confidence. When you review the list of common causes, one or both of the following should surface for you: (1) You are sabotaging your own self-confidence, or (2) Other people in your life, now or in the past, have done a good job of robbing it from you. You're going to learn what to do and how to do it when it comes to rebuilding confidence after years of negative input from yourself, and in many cases, from other well-meaning people.

> "Nobody can make you feel inferior without your consent."
> – Eleanor Roosevelt

"Know thyself" is all about knowing who we are and, more importantly, who we are not. It's a fun and rewarding exercise when you think about it. Fun because you'll see the humor in those times you tried being someone you're not. Rewarding because you'll discover a freedom you've not had before, and your confidence will soar when you understand that being you is all you need. You can stop being disingenuous, a fake and a fraud — or worse, a constant people-pleaser trying relentlessly to jump through ever-moving hoops.

Being the best you can be with your skills, abilities and talents will take you anywhere you want to go in life. You may lack some essential skill sets to get there, but those can be learned, as we'll discuss later in the book.

How do you discover who you really are? How do you remove years of negative input occupying space in your brain? Remember from the first chapter that negative input from experience is taking up valuable space needed for positive input. But you can make the positive push the negative out. It won't happen overnight, but it will happen.

Picture your brain as a cup. That cup is full of water, with water representing all the negative input you've received over the years. Then we have a pile of gold nuggets — that represents positive input. As you put gold nuggets into the cup of water, they push the water out. One by one, each gold nugget placed in the cup displaces water. There's very little water left when the cup is full of gold nuggets.

The good, positive stuff, the confidence-building tools and actions, will push the negative out, too. We're imperfect human creatures. Like a cup full of gold nuggets, there will be a small amount of water left (some negativity) but not enough to hurt you or others. It is as simple as that.

Oh, Yes You Can! Action: Find a cup and fill it with water. Place it in a bowl big enough to collect the overflow of water. Then using marbles or some other item to represent gold nuggets, start placing them in the cup, and state out loud what each nugget represents as a positive in your life. Whenever you're feeling low, repeat this exercise.

The first gold nugget in your full cup of water is going to be knowing yourself. Who are you without negative influences from others? When most of us are asked who we are, about ourselves, we typically answer with what we do in our work life, at home or on the job. That is not who we are. That's what we do.

Think about it for a few moments. There are many answers other than what you do in your job or your role at home. Remove activities and past training when you think of who you are or even who you want to be. Think in terms of giving and receiving. If you had nothing to give but a part of yourself to another, what would you give? If you were to receive from another, not money or anything material, what would you want to receive? What could you give and what would you want to receive that didn't include money or a material thing? Your answer to these questions will offer an important clue to who you really are.

Oh, Yes You Can! Action: Put your answers to paper. Write them down. Stare at the paper and think. Chances are, you'll discover who you are and who you would like to become if you knew what skills you needed to become that person. You may also discover what it is you could become passionate about, if you don't already know. You will find clues to your significance in this lifetime. If you can think it, if you can imagine it, you either have it already or have the ability to acquire the meaning you search for in life.

After you've finished your list, consider other people, not to compare yourself but to identify qualities you'd like to acquire or become more skilled in. Chances are that if you admire and respect others for qualities they have, you have those qualities yourself. There just may be too much negative input occupying brain space for you to see it; it's just useless clutter, like junk in the garage you don't need or want. Or, you may just not know how to show the real you; you may lack the skills you need to make that seed germinate into a flower.

The next thing you do is talk with trusted and supportive friends or family, even your boss or co-workers, if you trust them and they've demonstrated that they support you. Ask them what qualities and attributes they see in you that they admire, like and respect. What have they observed about you? What stands out above all else? Don't blow it off if you're not good at receiving compliments. Just thank them and add it to your list.

You're not looking for people to tell you what you should or shouldn't do. What you want is to know what stand-out qualities you have that they've observed. You'll figure out what you should or shouldn't do in time. That's not important right now.

What you will discover is that who we are leads us to many options and opportunities in life. It's when we get stuck on what we do that our options become limiting, and for some, depressing, if we don't like what we've trained for or settled for. Rebuilding confidence is about options and opportunities that are a good fit for who you are or want to become.

> *"What lies behind us and what lies before us are tiny matters compared to what lies within us."*
> – Ralph Waldo Emerson

By now, you should be feeling a little more confident, a little better about yourself. Before long, you will have far more confidence. But you're beginning to push out the negativity

— the confidence-sabotaging attitudes and the low self-worth. Those nuggets of good stuff are replacing years of damaging input.

By focusing on who you are while you're doing what you do (at work or other activities, including parenting, personal and social relationships), watch body language and listen to the people who are surrounding you. Pay attention to and notice how they respond to you.

What were you doing or saying when you noticed or heard a change in their body language or tone of voice? Are they happier, more comfortable or trusting of you? Have you inspired them? Have you given them reason to have confidence and know you're supportive of them? Maybe they came to you with a problem, and you helped them solve it or directed them to people who could. It could be that you just listened with intent to understand, not to criticize or condemn. It could be that you shared a good laugh together. It could be any number of things. Just be more observant and add those feel-goods to your list.

And too, there may be times when you just blow it. We all do. There are times when we say things we shouldn't and have attitudes we and those around us don't like. The goal is to reduce the number of occurrences and learn and grow from those times. If it calls for an apology, be willing to give one immediately. It's never too late to acknowledge and express appreciation — something as simple as a thank you when someone says something nice or does something kind, however small, that they didn't have to do.

> ***Oh, Yes You Can! Tip:*** *There's no reason for holding on to guilt or bad feelings when an apology says a lot about your character to the one receiving it. Guilt serves one purpose — to alert us that we have shortcomings. Don't wait to right a wrong, and don't let guilt take up brain space needed for the good stuff. We can learn from our shortcomings. We all have them.*

Do you realize that not all shortcomings or weaknesses we have require fixing? As long as the weakness doesn't negatively impact or hurt us or others and is not a big deal to us, it doesn't require fixing if we don't want to expend the energy on it. It's just another freedom gained from knowing yourself. There are a lot of things we don't do well and don't need to do well. If it doesn't hurt us or anyone else, it really doesn't matter.

The important piece is that you know who you are, know who you are not, and know what you want to improve upon based on what you've discovered with the exercises in this book.

One more thing before you turn to the next chapter — start giving gold nuggets away to others, everyday in some way. Say, do and be the person who not only receives the feel goods but gives them away. It can't be money or anything material. Just some of that feel-good stuff. Share it, and it will be shared with you!

C H A P T E R F I V E

Power Building

We can't achieve sustainable confidence without relationships — good relationships. But how do we determine the
difference between a good relationship and a bad one? Our
childhood comes to mind. There were some kids we were
told we couldn't or shouldn't play with. They were "a bad
influence," our parents warned, and nothing good was
going to come from being friends or playing with them. The
same is true for us now. Some people are good influences
while others are not. As we seek to sort through who is good
for us and who is not, we need to be brutally honest with
ourselves. A couple of things come into play.

> *"Personal power is the ability to achieve what you want.*
> *More than anything else, it is personal power that brings*
> *you success and happiness."*
> – Frederick Mann

An easy way to figure out who is a good influence and who is
not is to look back at the last twelve months. Think of this
exercise as another cup filled with water. If you visualize
holes in the bottom of your cup, each hole would represent a

negative influence. These people drain you of energy, constantly criticize you and negatively impact your self-worth and confidence.

They may even be dream-stealers — people who are always telling you that something won't work or you can't do something, rather than helping you explore how to make it work and find a way to do it. Some of these folks might be family, friends or coworkers you've had for years. If so, you may not be able to put a lot of distance between you and them.

You can, however, prepare and protect yourself when you're around them. Love may run deep between you, as it should between family and close friends. We're not talking about loving or not loving. It's all about sustaining confidence and your sense of well-being now and into your future. If they are negative and destructive, they represent holes in your cup, with or without love.

If you have a number of negative influences in your life, imagine how many holes you must have in your cup! No matter how fast you fill your cup with the good stuff, the encouraging and positive things, there are too many drain holes to hold it. Your cup will drain faster than you can fill it.

Oh, Yes You Can! Action: Create a list of confidence robbers and negative influences who drain you. Identify the ones you can let go of or remove from your life. Each one you remove plugs a hole, slowing the drain of the good stuff. The goal is to have the positive influences and events spill over from your cup. The sooner you plug the majority of the holes, the faster you'll reach your goal of becoming a confident and significant person in your life and in the lives of others.

Creating the list can be easy. Taking action on the list to remove the negative influences can be a bit of a challenge. Keep in mind, there will always be a couple of drain holes. Life is not perfect, nor are we. Besides, you may choose to keep a friend or two who have little negative impact on you, but who don't offer much on the positive side either. They may just be likeable and fun to be around sometimes.

For those negative influences you can't remove from your life, limit your contact and the types of conversations you have with them. It's not always possible, but if you can establish some boundaries with the person, what works for you and what doesn't, do it. Let them know the impact some of their words or actions have on you, and in turn, what it does to your attitude toward them when hurtful words or behaviors are thrust at you.

> *"The way you treat yourself sets the standard for others."*
> – Sonya Friedman

There are also those times when you have no option but to listen to them rant. If it's not constructive, either count to yourself or mentally recite the ABCs to keep their negativity from being absorbed in your brain — don't let it take up space. Often times, coworkers, parents or even a spouse may not respect your needs, but are still people you just can't close out of your life. They will be among your drain holes, but you can limit the amount of their drain on you. Shrink the hole. If you don't react or engage in the negative bantering, they will often shift their aim onto another target.

You've now identified which holes you can plug by removing or distancing the negative people in your life. For the others, you'll shrink the size of the hole they create by keeping your guard up, tuning them out or just learning to manage their negative influence more effectively.

> ***Oh, Yes You Can! Tip:*** *It's not enough to just identify the confidence-robbers and negative influences in your life. You have to act on it! It will take a lot of strength to rid yourself of certain people or things in your life. You can do it!*

Congratulations! You're making progress and exercising your personal power, putting you well on your way to re-building your confidence.

Now focus on your good, positive influences — the confidence boosters. They are the people who keep your cup filled with good. In time, virtually all of the negative input taking up space in your brain will be replaced with their positive input and influence. They may not all stand out as your closest, most continual resource for encouragement, but they don't create more holes. They don't drain you. You may only have one or two people who stand out as trusted, dependable resources of support and encouragement. One is all you need, but more is better.

All those you've listed as part of your positive-influence team will be people with whom you want to spend most of your time – they do no harm. And too, it's important that you become a person who returns encouragement and support to those giving it to you and to others, like you, who need it.

Everyone you come in contact with in life has a cup, too. Most people have more drain holes than they can manage. Make sure you're not part of their drain. If you don't know how to become a positive, encouraging and supportive influence on others, observe people who are. Don't compare yourself negatively; just learn from them. Duplicate what they do, and it will become, slowly, who you are. You'll possess the same qualities as those you admire and who support you. If you're saying to yourself right now that it's not you, then commit to making it you.

Let's summarize how to best make this work for you. You need to make three lists. First, list all those relationships we call "keepers." They are good influences and confidence-boosters in our lives. Our standard of behavior, our attitude and thoughts are positive and optimistic when we're engaged with them. They inspire and exude hope in the present and for the future. You feel confident and secure when in their midst and after you have connected with them. You may want to add a person or two who you just enjoy being around; they don't add a lot, but they don't take away either. They do no harm to your spirit, mentally or emotionally. They fill a need, so you add them to this list.

Your next list will be those people who may not be positive influences but just can't be removed from your life. These are people you will have to be on guard with when you're around them. You'll have to work on finding a way to minimize their destructive attitudes and behaviors when in their presence. They are also people who either create problems or become part of a problem. Little makes them happy, and they have no desire to change.

Your final list will be those people you must distance yourself from entirely. You don't need to slam the door on them, but you must not delay in separating yourself from their negative influence. They are drain holes in your cup and have a negative effect on the good stuff, draining it so fast you can't sustain or hold onto it. You can't replace the negative input stored in your brain with positive, confidence-building habits by continuing to surround yourself with their influence.

Finally, check your list daily. Add and move people onto the correct lists as you gain more confidence and become more aware of the impact each individual has on you. Draw lines through those people you have removed from your life. The reason you'll be moving some people from list to list is simple. Life happens; events and circumstances change people. You will change by reading this book. Some who were listed as negative may change and become a positive influence. Others may turn negative for any number of reasons. Some people just weren't meant to be in your life for an extended period of time. Your lists will change as you and others change.

CHAPTER   SIX

Skill Building

You've learned several things by now. You know that you had a lot of confidence as a toddler and how your brain works by storing input and taking in what you expose it to. You've discovered that finding the origin or cause of low confidence is essential to rebuilding confidence. And you know how important it is to be surrounded by good influences. Now it's time to learn the soft skills you will need to sustain confidence and develop a good relationship with yourself and with those who will support and encourage you along the way.

Success in anything we do takes skills. We don't consciously think about most of the skills we use. You've most likely never thought about some of these skills you have as "learned skills," but all skills are that. If you've ever wondered what the real secret to success is, the secret is mastering essential skills.

These are the skills underlying all the actions you must take to do something well. That is why so many people try so hard to make life work and still feel like failures. It takes knowing which skills to develop, how to use them and how to use them effectively. Knowing what to do without knowing how to do it well will end in disappointment and failure.

Some skills will be easy to learn on your own. Others will require observing or learning from someone who easily demonstrates mastery of the skill. They can teach you or show you how to use the skill effectively to achieve the outcomes you want or need.

> *"Just as much as we see in others, we have in ourselves."*
> – William Hazlitt

For example, problem solving is a skill. If you're not a very good problem solver, don't just avoid trying to solve problems. Learn the steps to good problem solving. Then seek out someone who has mastered this skill. Ask them to help you. Observe how they explore the origin of the real problem versus focusing on fixing a symptom.

Focusing on symptoms will not fix a problem. It will resurface time and again. Watch how they progress through the steps — how they identify who the stakeholders are, who is affected by the problem and the solution. You'll learn a lot about the process and how to make it work for you. You must become a student, though; you must observe and participate in numerous problem-solving experiences to understand how to apply the skills in many different circumstances.

Asking for help is a sign of intelligence. Don't hesitate. Resisting help from reliable sources when you need it is counterproductive and won't help you develop the skills you need to succeed.

First, let's look at the skill sets you'll need to rebuild your confidence and achieve personal power. In the next chapter, you'll learn the skill sets that successful people use to succeed: the secrets of how they do it.

Self-Discipline: It will take self discipline to shed the negative influences in your life and to deal effectively with those negative influences you can't shed. You'll need that discipline to consistently demonstrate that you, too, are a person who is a positive and an inspiring influence on others in all aspects of life.

Oh, Yes You Can! Action: Commit the motto "Do It Now" to memory, and use it to replace that space in your brain that has been filled with procrastination mantras. Push procrastination thoughts out, and "do it now" will take their place.
Becoming proficient in the skills you need to learn will also take self-discipline until it becomes natural for you.

Problem Solving: Life happens. There are problems we have to deal with on a daily basis. It doesn't matter whether you call them issues or challenges, they are problems needing a fix, or at the very least, needing to be managed successfully. Learn the steps to problem–solving; observe good and bad problem solvers and practice to become more skillful. You'll get people's attention in a positive way if you focus on finding solutions instead of whining about problems. The people you want to attract into your support and inspiration circle as friends are problem solvers. Whiners are just holes in the bottom of other people's cups. They may still think that whining is a character trait to be proud of, but those who have to listen to them know better. Whining children are bad enough; whining adults are worse.

Decision Making: Decisions are a part of our everyday life from the time we decide to get out of bed to the time we go back to bed. We are making decisions all day long. Most of them we give little or no thought to; they're routine. However, many decisions we make require thought and input from others. Rebuilding confidence, filling our cup with those gold nuggets, means we need to pay attention to our decisions and their consequences, whether good or bad. Each good decision and good outcome will add another nugget to your cup. Learn how, the process of making good decisions and choices, and then watch your confidence grow. You will be astounded by the respect you receive from others.

One key to good decision making is having the wisdom to look at both the best and worst that can result from the decision, and who it will impact. Ask others who have made similar decisions about their thoughts and outcomes; do your homework and get the facts before you make the decision. And for those of you who believe it's a weakness to ask others for input or advice, it's not. It's being smart. Thinking you have all the answers can be dangerous and self-defeating.

Observation: This is a skill that will accelerate your confidence if you use it to your advantage. There is no better way to learn more about ourselves and others, including what does and doesn't work, than observing. You observe yourself to determine what areas you need to work to improve as well as those things you do well and need to do more of. Observe how your attitude and behaviors affect you and others. Observe others to understand how their attitude and behaviors affect you and others — not to compare yourself to them, but to learn.

You'll also want to observe how other people react to your behavior, words and tone of voice. Is it a positive, negative or just neutral response? You can learn a lot about how good, solid confidence influences you and others. You will also observe how arrogance (not the same as confidence by any means) negatively influences people. Arrogance actually demonstrates a lack of confidence — it is a smoke screen.

True confidence, as you will observe, isn't arrogant. With true confidence, there's no need for arrogance.

Listening: Listen carefully to yourself talk. And listen carefully to others. Listen to what you say and how you say it. Combine listening with observing, and you'll discover the impact your words, thoughts and behaviors have on you and other people. When you learn to ask appropriate questions, listen with the intent to learn and do not speak without purpose, you'll find people are attracted to you. You are listening in order to understand yourself and them. If you see another individual as being the most important thing in the room and listen without distraction, you'll gain confidence in your ability to meet new people. You will also become more valued in whatever work you do or relationships you want to develop.

> *Oh, Yes You Can! Tip: The next time you find yourself engaged in conversation with someone, listen intently to what they have to say. Don't make it about you, make it all about them. Don't let your mind wander or dwell on how you will respond — just listen. You'll be amazed at how much more gratifying the conversation will be. You may even find that someone who once irritated you by controlling a conversation really has some worthwhile things to say.*

Speaking: Using your observation and listening skills, pay attention to how people talk, the words they use and the things they talk about. How we speak and what we speak about tells a lot about us. It reveals our level of trust for people; whether or not we're controlling, abusive, blaming or apologetic; and even if we are unsure of ourselves or our topic.

The words we use also reveal a lot. If our words are inappropriate, highly critical and judgmental or if they are inspiring, uplifting, positive and optimistic, what do they reveal about our character? Is it ideas, concepts and/or making a contribution to the greater good, or mere idle gossip? Is it about finding solutions to a problem or just complaining about a problem? Practice thinking about what you want to say, how you want to say it and the message you want the listener to hear. Make your conversations purposeful, and let them reflect who it is you want to be and how you want to be valued.

Reading and Writing: Reading provides knowledge; knowledge is power. It gives us the power to converse with people well and to learn from the mistakes and successes of others. Good writing skills are essential. Use the words that will mean what you want to convey to the reader. Abbreviations for words used in text messages and emails are not considered good writing skills. If the message you want to convey is important and requires you to be perceived well, write with care and avoid the abbreviations.

Accountability and Personal Responsibility: Blaming others is another example of an attitude that gets you nowhere. Nothing is learned and no respect is given by blaming other people for your own errors in judgment, mistakes or failures. Shifting blame, and failing to own up to one's involvement or culpability, will lead to a repeat performance of the mistake. It's only when we acknowledge our errors and seek to take appropriate action to right a wrong, that we avoid repeating the mistakes.

People most respected are those who acknowledge their slip-ups, change their attitude and behavior, and demonstrate a willingness to learn from experience. Keep in mind that most people know the truth and aren't buying the excuses anyway. Failing to own up is a sure way to lose confidence, respect and support from those important people on your support team.

Trust and Honesty: Trusting and being trustworthy and honest are essential to a strong support team and to your self-confidence. Being honest with yourself and others and surrounding yourself with like people is the foundation of lifelong, rewarding relationships. You may end up with only a handful of really good people, but it's better to have a handful of good people than a lot of bad influences surrounding you. If others in your support team are not open, honest and trustworthy with you, explore why. As with accountability and personal responsibility, if the reasons have nothing to do with your attitude or behaviors, move that person off your list of supporters onto one of the other lists. If the reasons have to do with you, determine whether it's something you need to work on or improve.

"Life shrinks or expands in proportion to one's courage."
– Anais Nin

Courage: This is a skill we usually think of in the context of doing something heroic, like jumping in the water to save a drowning person. Many of us have burdens and challenges we never could have imagined. Instead of walking away from them, try walking into them. Winston Churchill once said, "When you're walking through hell, keep walking." Whether it's changing an attitude or behavior; forging new, supportive and rewarding friendships; letting go of those people who drain you; testing your new confidence level with something new; doing something you've always wanted to do but were afraid to do imperfectly at first; or apologizing to someone, life takes courage to adapt to change and the need for change.

Rebuilding your confidence takes courage. Is that any less courageous than jumping in the water to save someone? No. In fact, it may be more courageous to plan and act upon rebuilding your confidence. Often it takes more courage to let go of old, harmful attitudes and behaviors, and to commit to learning and practicing new skills, than it does to perform the actions we typically think of as courageous.

You're now well on your way to achieving a confidence level you may never have thought possible. If something is not working for you or your confidence is slipping away, review these skills to see which one you may have neglected to use.

C H A P T E R   S E V E N

Critical Thinking

Let's define "successful." Being successful means you are doing exactly what you want to do with your life. You know what to do, how to do it, and how to do it well. It may be that you want to become a highly successful bricklayer or you want to own your own successful business. It could be that you want to be a highly successful parent. As long as it's honorable and legal, you get to define successful on your terms.

Unfortunately, most of us aren't doing what we want to do, and there are things we'd like to change. It may be that we feel stuck in a job or relationship that doesn't make us happy. Perhaps there's a dream we've always had that we're no closer to fulfilling than we were a decade or two ago. Maybe we want to change how we feel, our attitudes and emotions, or how we think and react. Perhaps we want to change how we interact with others, or change some character trait. Maybe we've worked hard to achieve success and haven't quite reached the level of success we truly desire. Maybe it's just that life isn't working for us.

If that's you, read on. You may know what you need to do to succeed; this chapter and the next three are going to talk about how to do it. We're going to discuss skill sets that successful people excel in. Success isn't achieved by just revving up your enthusiasm and telling yourself that you can do it. Practical skills are required. We all have them latent within us, but they need to be cultivated. Successful people know this, and have worked to develop these essential skills. Working together, these skills generate success.

> *"Success is going from failure to failure without losing your enthusiasm."*
> – Winston Churchill

The secret to anyone's success is embedded in soft skills. They are the skills we use to make anything work for us. Success is not dependent on what you do but on how well you do it. You must have these skills to succeed in anything you choose to do. And, you must know how to use them effectively.

There are four categories on which you'll need to focus. Remember, no one is perfect, and each of us, including highly successful people, have strengths and weaknesses. We get in a rut when we try to be all things to all people or believe we must be good in all skill areas. We only have to be smart enough to know ourselves. We need only know which skills we use well, which we can become masters of or proficient in, and which we will need to learn or improve. We may also have to recognize the need to have others assist us with learning and mastering some skill sets.

Many of the skills in this section could be ones you know and know how to use effectively. There are others that you will need to work on. You won't do all of them well. Just focus on the ones you know you need to learn or improve on. Refer to and review this chapter to identify which skills worked for you, and if something didn't turn out well for you, which ones you may have neglected or need to practice.

Oh, Yes You Can! Action: As you read this chapter, identify your skill strengths and weaknesses — those of importance to you. Focus on the skill sets that are most important to attaining your immediate goals. Skills have been assigned categories. It helps you understand their application — what and how they relate to what you're doing or trying to achieve. Keep a list for each category and the appropriate skills needed.

However, the skill categories are interdependent. That is, when working on a particular category, you'll likely use many skills from the other categories. In time, you'll figure out which category is most challenging to you. It may be emotion management. You may do well in all other categories, but when emotions come into play, you let them get out of control. Focus your energies on learning and practicing those skill sets that you find most challenging.

With that, let's begin with the first skill set, critical thinking:

Skill Set #1: Critical Thinking Skills

Critical Thinking: These skills are used almost daily by everyone, although some of these skills are used more often than others. The quality of our lives depends on our ability to use critical-thinking skills effectively.

Solving problems, making good decisions, negotiating, conflict management and all the communication skills are critical to our well-being and that of others. Our relationships, employment, finances, health, safety and security in life are in some way dependent on critical thinking. Learning, practicing, and becoming skilled in our thinking is a necessity if we expect to manage life with less crisis and chaos and with more confidence and success.

A. Problem Solving: If we are not skilled in solving problems, it's important to find a supporter who is and to learn from that person. Successful people don't ignore problems or hide from them. They have learned to move into them and solve them in order to get closer to their goals. Hiding, ignoring problems, or hoping they'll go away is naïve at best; more likely, it's being stuck in a state of denial. Focusing on the symptom doesn't fix the problem. It will return until solved. Learn the steps to good problem solving and get experienced help if you don't know how to solve the problems you're facing.

B. Decision Making: Achieving success requires making good decisions. Not every decision you make will be a good one, so part of good decision-making is having a damage-control plan if a decision doesn't turn out well. Anticipate the worst that can happen if things don't work out as planned, and know ahead of time what you can do to fix the situation. Then act fast and move on toward your goal. Not reaching out for experienced and trusted help when you need it can result in self-sabotage. Failing, then feeling sorry for self, afraid to make decisions or failing to take some risk, is self-defeating. Successful people fail to make the right decisions all the time, too. But they move on, consult with others, get as much input as they can and continue to make decisions, better ones each time. They surround themselves with their support team, take what they've learned and move on — smarter, wiser and better-informed for the next time. The only reason to look back is to avoid repeating the same mistakes. Always look at what worked and where a decision may have been flawed. That's how we learn.

C. Negotiating: This is something we do daily. Often we think of negotiating as a business skill, but we're engaged in it at home, socially and on the job, whatever that job may be. Many of our conversations involve negotiating. Those of us with children spend most of our waking hours negotiating with them. Successful people learn this skill from practice. Some negotiations are win/win; others focus not on a trade but simply an offer of good will to another without expecting anything in return. The best advice about negotiating is that all take and no give is a sure way to fail. Successful people know that quality of life and success are dependent on "we" not "me." No one succeeds alone. Being stubborn or feeling entitled at the expense of another is not a recipe for success.

D. Conflict Resolution or Management: This is a critical-thinking skill that's vital to our success. Conflicts are part of life. Each of us sees the world and our surroundings through our life experiences and acquired knowledge. No two people are the same, and disagreements will happen. Conflicts don't have to be confrontational, ugly or in your face. Many conflicts can never be resolved, and there is not necessarily anything wrong with that. Agreeing to disagree is not resolving anything; it falls into the category of managing. Successful people know that if something can't be resolved and there can be no meeting of the minds, the only thing left to do is manage the disagreement well. Managing conflict well requires understanding and meeting the needs of both people when possible. Being stubborn and unwilling to compromise or serve the greater good of those involved can produce even greater conflict.

E. Listening: Successful people are good listeners. They ask questions and listen with the intent to learn. They learn from others' successes, but they also learn a lot from others' failures. When asking for help, they listen and ask follow-up questions to make sure they understood the meaning of the answer or instructions. There is a wealth of knowledge to be gained from listening to other people and asking questions.

F. Speaking: Think before you speak. We mentioned in an earlier chapter that you should learn to speak purposefully. Know what you want to say and learn to frame it so the listener understands what you want them to hear. It takes practice, but you'll see the results pretty quickly. Listeners will respond positively. They won't have to search for the meaning, and walk away wondering what you meant or misunderstanding your intent. Pay attention to your tone of voice, and make sure it's one that is respectful and inspiring.

G. Reading and Writing: Read to understand, and write to be understood. Always read what you've written to make sure the reader will understand your point and that you will be respected. Don't use inappropriate language. Be respect-ful, and don't use text message abbreviations or emoticons if it's a business communication and you're seeking respect. If reading is not your strength and comprehension is difficult, read more! The only way to improve comprehension and speed is to do more reading.

> ***Oh, Yes You Can! Tip:*** *If there is disagreement or conflict when emotions are involved, give the situation 24 hours before responding. Write the letter or message now and put it to the side until the next day when emotions have subsided. Read it again before sending to make sure it's really what you want to say.*

CHAPTER EIGHT

Emotion Management

In the last chapter, we said that no skill category was independent of the other three. We need to use skills from each category to be successful in all categories. For example, emotion management is critical in solving problems, making good decisions, negotiating or in any communication skill. If we don't know how to manage our emotions, our emotions can, and usually do, negatively impact our ability to do anything else well.

If we look back at our past successes and failures, emotions have played a key role in outcomes. Even in something as elementary as learning to ride a bike or learning to read, our success was the result of managing our emotions. When we became frustrated and angry after trying and failing to get it right away, we calmed down. By managing our emotions, we didn't quit trying. We stayed with it until we succeeded.

As adults, virtually everything we do, every event in our life, any interaction with people at work or at home, will cause an emotional response. We experience happiness, sadness, frustrations, anger, fear, peace, confusion, overwhelm and despair for any number of reasons. How we react and respond with our emotions, how we manage them, will determine how good or bad the outcomes will be. When we come across people stuck in the past, unable to get beyond a negative event or even a positive one, they haven't managed their emotions well. This is the present, and we must live in it or get left behind. Denial is another example of unmanaged emotions. What is, is. The sooner we manage our emotions and deal with reality, the sooner we get on with life.

The key to managing our emotions, as many successful and confident people know, is to do it skillfully. We all have these skills within us, waiting to be cultivated. Harm occurs when emotions are unmanaged or out of control. We can lose precious opportunities if we allow this. How do we know when that happens?

The first sign is that we recognize an inner tension building. That's our signal to stop or contain, think or reflect, and assess or process the situation. Most often we will discover before responding or reacting poorly that the situation doesn't deserve the rising intensity we're giving it. Successful people pay attention to their reactions and responses. They know big opportunities can disappear in a heartbeat if they say or do something based not in logic, but in negative or out of controlled emotional reaction.

The older we get, the more attuned we are to our gut instinct. There is justification to listening to that. And there is also justification for questioning it. The more life experiences we have, good and bad, the more reliable our instinct becomes. But successful people seldom rely on their gut instinct alone in making decisions. They consult others with more knowledge and experience; they seek factual data, use logic to determine best and worse case scenarios, process all information and then decide what they will do and how they will do it.

Learn which skills control emotions and start to become aware of them when the inner tension begins to heighten. Stop, reflect and process. If reflecting and processing is unfamiliar to you, seek out someone from your support team to talk to about the situation. That will give you a chance to hear someone else reflect and process with you.

Skill Set # 2: Emotion Management Skills

> *"You can conquer almost any fear if you will only make up your mind to do so. For remember, fear doesn't exist anywhere except in the mind."*
> – Dale Carnegie

A. Manage Fear and Anxiety: Successful people have fears and anxieties just like you and the rest of the world. The difference is that they have learned to manage them. They move into them, not away from them. Some fears can be overcome completely. Other fears and anxiety-causing situations never go away. Successful people learn not to let them take control. Their fears don't stop them from doing what they have to do. If you're having trouble managing fear and anxiety, talk with a trusted supporter. Ask for their help. Often just talking with someone helps minimize the fears. Then identify the skills you need to master in order to prevent these emotions from ruining your life and robbing you of a deserved future. Taking action, moving into the fear, and asking for help is exactly what successful people do or have done. Unmanaged fear and anxiety can damage our well-being, cause depression and lost opportunities.

Courage is essential for success in anything. Although successful people make it appear easy, the truth is that they, too, struggled and had to dig deep to find the courage to move through their fears and failures. Once they found the courage to take action, they found it wasn't as difficult as they thought it was going to be. Dreading taking action is worse than actually taking action. It takes courage to do what is not easy or outside our comfort zones. The thrill of victory is found in finally taking the necessary action.

B. Manage Stress: Stress at a low to medium level is not problematic. It's when it gets out of control or reaches a high intensity for a period of time that it can do harm. Successful people live with stress in their lives, high stress at times, but know how to control it. Some reduce stress by exercising or taking needed time do something relaxing that they enjoy. When you feel overwhelmed, try putting your problem-solving and decision-making skills to work. Successful people are no different than anyone else; they've just learned the skill sets to better manage stress. They don't let it get out of control and cause harm to themselves or others with inappropriate attitudes or behaviors. They may appear calm, but behind the scenes there is usually a lot going on. They also know how to delegate and ask for help if their plate is too full.

C. Manage Anger: This is another skill that is misunderstood by many. Anger is a healthy emotion as long as it is never used destructively. Successful people seldom harbor anger, either toward themselves or another, for mistakes or failures. They deal with it, learn from it and move on. Forgiveness is one of the greatest gifts we can give to ourselves and others; it is also one of the greatest gifts we can receive. Use it more often to find more peace within. Successful people look inward first to identify what role they played in whatever made them angry. They seek to learn from situations that bring anger rather than looking for someone to blame. Forgive yourself, forgive others and ask for forgiveness when needed.

D. Manage Adversity (loss/grief/disappointment/failure): Life happens, and life is not fair. It just is what it is. We must learn to deal with the cards we're dealt. Successful people have their share of adversity, too. Often they have far more of it than we could ever imagine. The difference is that they have accepted it as part of life and use the skills they've learned to cope with and manage it as it comes. They understand that life happens whether we're prepared for it or not. You, too, can deal with adversity skillfully and with grace. It just takes using the right skills to get through it and staying connected to your support team.

If you're experiencing emptiness, a "negative inner tension", as Charles R. Wang, M.D. identifies it, from adversities or life's challenges, you can also successfully manage or eliminate it by focusing on plugging the holes in your cup. Decrease the negative influences and increase the positive ones. Learn to manage your emotions skillfully, and use these skills to build better, stronger and more supportive relationships. Having a good support system will get you through virtually anything in life.

> *"The courage to be is the courage to accept oneself,*
> *in spite of being unacceptable."*
> – Paul Tillich

E. Manage Procrastination: The easiest way to manage procrastination is to catch yourself procrastinating and repeat out loud, "Do It Now!" This has worked for virtually everyone who remembers to do it. If it's important and must be done, doing it now eliminates guilt and regret and reduces tomorrow's burdens.

F. Manage Time: (prioritize and organize): These are difficult skills for a lot of people. Time flies, and we never seem to find enough of it. Emotions play a big role in time management, prioritizing and organizing. When we let our emotions control us, we lose control over all three skills. When we become overwhelmed, logic, clear thinking and good judg-ment tend to get lost in the chaos. All three of these skills are essential for success. Without control over these areas, chaos will rule our lives. Some things are important, and others are not. Learn to know the difference. Do what's important, and do it now.

G. Manage Finances: Many people allow their emotions to control their finances. Reckless disregard for financial responsibilities has no good ending. Successful people use their critical-thinking and emotion-management skills to manage their finances and spending. If you are impulsive or compulsive with money, get out of your own way and seek a trusted, proven support team member to assist and/or monitor, or even control your spending and money management. Don't expect different results from doing the same thing over and over while sinking deeper and deeper into financial problems.

"Be clear about your goal, but be flexible about the process of achieving it."

– Brian Tracy

H. Flexibility/Adaptability: The inability to be flexible or to adapt to change is emotionally draining and negatively impacts critical-thinking skills. Successful people have learned to be flexible and adapt swiftly to change. Flexibility does not mean compromising your values. It simply means letting go of stubbornness if it is not serving your best interest, your objectives, or other people. Successful individuals realize that the world is changing constantly. Those refusing to adapt will be left behind. Flexibility and adaptability will keep you healthier; it doesn't take as much energy to deal with life when you can adapt to the changes you face.

C H A P T E R   N I N E

Relationships

Each skill category is vital to your success. In order to build good, healthy and rewarding relationships and interact successfully in all social settings, you will need your critical-thinking skills and emotion-management skills. All relationships in our personal and work life succeed or fail based on how well or how poorly we use these skills. We must practice them everyday until we become skilled and successful using them and no longer have to think about it—until they have become part of us.

If your parents told you, as a child, not to play with someone because they were a bad influence and would give you a bad reputation, they were right. The same applies to all of us as adults. Like it or not, we are judged by the company we keep. If we hang out with chronic complainers and criticizers, we become one. If we hang out with untrustworthy people, we're going to be known as untrustworthy too. If we associate with people who blame everyone and anyone for their chaotic lives, we will end up doing the same thing.

Successful people are very careful about who they associate with and call a friend. They know that it's far easier and faster to fall than it is to climb. If you work hard to get to where you want to go, you don't want others pulling you down.

How do we know that for fact? We've been there, done that. We've all made bad choices, for all the right or wrong reasons, and paid for it. Be wise with your selection of friends. If they don't share your values, don't get involved.

And, don't think your education alone will get you where you want to go. You may have a degree from the best college in the country, but without good relationships, it will fail you. Employment or business opportunities, promotions, good raises and bonuses are relationship-dependent. It doesn't matter what you know if you don't know how to do it and do it well, including building relationships.

How do you know you've done it and done it well? The quality of your relationships, how well you developed and nurtured them with bosses, coworkers, vendors and customers will dictate your level of success. If your career is not going the way you want it to, first look at your relationships. Are you forging good, rewarding ones? If not, why not? If it's a value issue, find employment with people who share your values.

It's a small world, as the saying goes. Our social connections — all those relationships outside of our work and immediate family life — are important too. How we relate to people, act and react in these settings, can open or close doors for us. This also applies to social networking on the Internet. Untold numbers of people have destroyed their credibility and lost friends and job opportunities because of their behavior in public or on the Internet social networks. The best advice we can give is to choose your friends and your actions carefully. Don't think bad or reckless behaviors, yours or your friends', won't come back to haunt you. They may and oftentimes do. People know people who know people who know us.

We've all heard people say they are self-made successes. That's simply not true. No one succeeds alone, but many people fail going it alone. People along our journey through life help us, share knowledge and information, give us ideas, support our efforts, believe in us, and introduce us to people who eventually help us get where we want to go. We never know who these people may be or where we'll meet them when they come into our lives. It's wise to be respectful, considerate and thoughtful to those who cross our paths, even strangers.

Our well-being, our happiness, is a direct reflection of our ability to develop and nurture good and rewarding relationships. It's never too late to start, and you will have all the tools you need to do it when you learn, practice and become skilled in relationship building.

Skill Set # 3: Relationship and Social Skills

A. Basic Courtesies: We've all seen successful people who act arrogant and lack basic courtesies. They are the exception, not the rule. Truly successful and confident people always remember where they came from and know who they are and who they are not. They are very respectful and mindful of other people, regardless of who they are, where they're from, the job they have, the car they drive or the house they live in. They understand that you should be respectful and mindful of those you pass on the way to the top, because if you encounter adversity, you pass them on the way down and may need their help. It's not smart to treat people as inferior or to think you're better or smarter than others.

B. Leadership: Leadership is a multi-faceted skill. Certainly, successful people exhibit mastery in leadership skills. However, it takes all the skills in this book plus more to be an effective leader of people. What many fail to realize is that leadership can be demonstrated in small ways every day. When highly successful people are asked who contributed to their success, most mention someone in their childhood or early adult years who played a big role in their development. Typically, it's someone in or close to the family or a mentor, educator or coach. Whoever those people were, they acted in a leadership capacity. To give encouragement, confidence, inspiration or hope to another human being is an act of leadership.

You may have heard that "to whom much has been given, much is expected." Giving back to society in even small ways is demonstrating leadership. Wherever you are and whatever you do, teaching, encouraging, inspiring, or helping another manage any part of life is your chance to lead. Setting an example for others to follow is also a demonstration of leadership. A good leader of people has learned, mastered and used all the skills we talk about here, every day and in all things.

C. Social Interaction: Interacting appropriately and well in social settings is a learned skill and vital to success. What most of us don't realize is that many successful people are, by nature, shy. They do what they have to and have learned the skills to do it well. The easiest way to begin to master social interaction is to learn to ask questions and listen, then ask another question.

If you take your eyes and thoughts off yourself and think only about making the people you're interacting with at ease and comfortable with you, you'll succeed in virtually any social situation. Social interaction is very stressful and uncomfortable when we fail to engage people well. When we get stuck on thinking about ourselves and what others are thinking about us, social interaction or networking is unsuccessful. Whether you're shy or outgoing, if you focus on asking questions and listening with interest, you'll become very skilled in social situations. You'll be comfortable anywhere.

D. Table Manners: Poor table manners can cost you dearly. Many good opportunities can be lost over bad table manners. Practice good table manners at home, and you'll not have to worry about forgetting them when it's important. Don't make the mistake of thinking it doesn't matter; it does.

Oh, Yes You Can! Tip: *Table manners are not just about using the right utensils or not talking with food in your mouth. Be respectful and courteous by not using your cell phone during a meal, particularly during a business meal. In fact, turn off all notifications and ringers. Give your undivided attention to those you are engaged with.*

E. Personal Grooming and Attire: Personal grooming is essential for successful people. It's not about where you shop or the label on your clothing. Basically, it's about cleanliness. Appropriate attire is dictated by the region you live in, the type of event you're attending, the people you'll be with and their attire. In some regions of the country, attire is more formal, while in others it is more casual. Extremely casual is seldom accepted as appropriate. This is another skill that requires the skill of observation. Observe others and duplicate, if appropriate. Try not to overdress or under-dress if the event is important to you. You must care about how you present yourself if you want to be successful.

F. Service to Others: Always seek to find ways you can be thoughtful and considerate of others' needs. Small acts of kindness are usually noticed in big ways. Use observation again to find ways to make someone else's day a better one. Whether opening a door, giving up a seat to someone in need, running an errand to help someone out or making a phone call to cheer someone up, there are many small ways to make a big difference in the lives of others. (You'll learn more about this skill in Chapter 11).

G. Teaming: Leading a team and being part of a team both require a host of skill sets. We can't think of one skill you wouldn't put to use. The challenge most people have in making teams work effectively is the understanding that virtually each team member has private motives or hidden agendas for being part of the team. If you know what those reasons are and if they can be met, teams won't end up in conflict or with a few doing the work of all. It takes open and honest communication between team members to reach objectives and goals without unnecessary tension.

H. Observation: We observe through all our senses, but primarily though our eyes and ears. Observing our surroundings and the people in it, up close or from a distance, can provide us with knowledge and insights we'd never learn in a classroom. To become a skilled observer, pay attention to your surroundings and the people around you, and talk with others about what they're observing. Successful people are very aware of these things. They look for how people behave. The words people use, their body language and reactions, speak volumes. We can learn a lot if we stop and pay attention.

It's also a great learning experience to observe oneself in different surroundings with different people; observing how you react, respond and behave in all kinds of situations gives you an awareness of what you might want to change. Sometimes changing small things makes a huge difference in how others see us or how well we project ourselves to others. Successful people have, over time, become highly skilled observers.

C H A P T E R   T E N

Character Building

You may learn, practice and become highly skilled in each of the three skill categories covered so far, but without character skills, none of the others will work well for you or be rewarding over the long haul. These skills are the compass we use to guide us through life. Character skills define us and are ultimately what generates our ability to respect ourselves and to be respected by others.

Character is about the essence of our being, our core values. Underestimating the importance of any one of these skills is common but not very smart. They are probably some of the hardest skills to consistently stay true to in all we do, especially when unwelcomed life events occur. It's those times when we make the choice to take the high road or travel the low road. It's been said that if we opt for the short-term gain, the easy or expeditious road, sell ourselves out, live a life of situation ethics, and do it just because it feels good, we'll suffer long-term pain. The pain is loss of respect and trust from those we most value.

And if we look back in our lives at valued relationships lost, virtually all the relationship problems were in some way connected to a failure in one or more of the character-building skill sets. Think about it. How many times have we stated or heard people talk about a failed relationship because of a trust or honesty issue?

Truly successful people take the high road. They stay true to their values even when it would be easier to forsake them for an instant reward. Achieving success takes having developed good, solid and dependable relationships, and sustaining relationships requires good character.

Character skills ensure the right people will be there for you when you need them and that you will be there for them in their time of need.

Skill Set # 4: Character-Building Skills

A. Accountability/Personal Responsibility: Successful people don't pass the blame. They look first at their role in any mishap or failure. They know that trust and respect are earned not by shifting blame but by owning what's theirs, acknowledging it, apologizing when appropriate and immediately, beginning the process of problem solving in order to move on. There is no learning and nothing to gain from shifting blame. The mistake will happen again if there's no accountability.

As you experience the respect gained by admitting your role and doing whatever is in your power to fix it, your confidence will be boosted. Refusing to be held accountable or resisting taking personal responsibility is the fastest way to lose your credibility with people who matter most in your life. Don't think people don't know the truth. You're usually the last one to discover that everyone knows it was you and not someone else. It's not worth the loss of trust, respect and future opportunities.

B. Commitment: Making commitments and honoring them builds confidence and self-worth. People will speak well of you when you keep your word. In the event you absolutely can't keep a commitment, make sure you inform those depending on you before the deadline. Failing to inform or make other arrangements when you can't keep a commitment can ruin your reputation. Learn to say "no" if asked to do something you know you can't do. Ask for help if you have overextended yourself. Successful people keep commitments or notify those involved that they cannot keep it, and make other acceptable arrangements. They don't ignore their obligations with the hope that no one will notice. Assuming that people don't keep track of unmet commitments or won't mind if you repeatedly fail to keep promises is a serious error in judgment.

> *"Repeat business or behavior can be bribed.*
> *Loyalty has to be earned."*
> – Janet Robinson

C. Loyalty: Always stay loyal to your core values — your ethics and morals — above all else. Compromising in these areas will only burden you with guilt and resentment. We live in a society that has tried to persuade us that loyalty to ourselves and our values can easily be compromised, and that compromise is justified when there's instant gratification or money in it. The wreckage from that belief is all around us, as the current economic situation reveals. It's short-term gain for long-term pain if you compromise your core values.

People who are successful in their personal and professional lives stay true to their core values, regardless of the circumstances. If you're experiencing the need to compromise your core values on the job, maybe it's time to find better employment or take the lead to set a new standard.

Loyalty to family and friends is the underpinning of good relationships and must be respected and given by all parties. Loyalty should never be violated unless valid evidence supports that it has been violated by others who don't value it. Loyalty to employer and coworkers is dependent on shared values. Giving it without receiving it is foolish. Loyalty is not a given or expectation unless it's earned.

D. Self Improvement/Personal Development: This is a daily activity for successful people. They know they don't have all the answers, are not anywhere near perfect and realize that learning is a lifelong activity. The world is rapidly changing; there is a wealth of knowledge out there and much to learn. We should never think we've arrived, that we know all there is to know and don't need to change or improve anything. It's been proven that those who need to change the most don't. Successful people make learning and personal development a lifelong commitment and make it a habit to practice self-improvement.

> *Oh, Yes You Can! Action: Make a contract with yourself to commit to continuous self-improvement. Clearly state your deliverables and the consequences for being in breach of contract. Reading and taking action from this book is first on the list — you're a step ahead already!*

E. Honesty/Integrity: Without honesty and integrity, rewarding relationships will be impossible. Genuine confidence will elude you. If we're not honest with ourselves, we can't be honest with others. Dishonesty in any relationship, with self or in personal or professional relationships, may cure short-term pain with a short-term gain, but it will always produce long-term pain. Few reputations are ever recovered after the discovery of dishonesty and deceit. Success is about moving forward, not cleaning up wreckage left behind by lack of good character. Believing that dishonesty won't be discovered is a fool's game, and we all know you're not a fool.

F. Trust/Trustworthiness: There is no greater honor than earning and having others place their trust in you. To be considered a trusted and trustworthy friend, family member, team member and coworker is a tribute to the quality of your character. What many fail to realize, yet successful people do, is that trust is not earned through a one-time event; it must be demonstrated constantly, every day and in all things. We are all human; we fail each other without intending to. When that occurs, forgiveness should follow. But when breaking a trust or being untrustworthy is habitual, that's a clear sign of a flawed character. Success, if any is achieved, will be fleeting if trust and trustworthiness are not held to a high standard and valued.

G. Diversity: This is a skill that is vital to our well-being in the world we live in today. No two people are the same. If we can't accept, respect and learn from others or appreciate our differences, we're narrow-minded. Closed minds and narrow minds can't make it in this world. If we are not receptive and willing to seek to understand another's culture, race, religion, disability, struggles or differences and we fail to realize our commonalities with one another, we become part of a bigger problem instead of a part of the solution. We should judge one another only by quality of character. The belief that your way is the only way can cause you to miss some important opportunities.

H. Supporting Others: If we want support, we need to learn to support others first. Many successful people will tell you that it's not as important what you know as who you know. Somewhere along the way, they imparted good will either by words they spoke or something they did for someone. They were remembered. You want to start having people collect good memories about you and how you were there for them. They'll be there for you at some point in your life.

In other words, supporting others is a critical and essential skill of your success strategy. It is also one of life's greatest pleasures that will lead to happiness. We've yet to meet genuinely happy people who focus solely on themselves. Supporting others is simply doing what is right to make this world a better place — making your contribution.

> *"Optimism is the faith that leads to achievement.*
> *Nothing can be done without hope and confidence."*
> – Helen Keller

I. Optimism/Positivity: What many people do not understand is that optimism and positivity are learned skills. And though you may not often hear it, it takes a host of other skill sets to sustain a positive, optimistic attitude. Imagine that you didn't know how to build good, healthy and rewarding relationships, but your future depended on them. How positive and optimistic could you possibly be? If you failed to succeed because you didn't have the skill sets, how long could you sustain positivity? You couldn't.

Imagine your problem-solving skills or decision-making skills weren't as good as they needed to be. How long would positivity and optimism last? If you knew what to do but couldn't figure out how to do it and do it well, how positive or optimistic about your present and future would you be? It takes many skills, all easy to learn, to sustain a positive and optimistic attitude. That's why, for many of us, positivity doesn't stick. We're not losers or failures. We just don't know which skills to use and how to use them effectively. Just thinking about optimism and positivity will not miraculously allow you to sustain a positive and optimistic attitude. You must have the right tools, starting with faith in yourself and be in motion rebuilding your confidence.

J. Respect: There are many forms of respect. There is respect for humanity, which is fundamental to good character. There is respect for our own property and that of others. There is respect for our natural resources and for future generations. There is respect for ourselves and others whom we love and care about and those we interact with, including in our work and social life.

Successful people understand a basic principle about respect: that first, we must respect ourselves. That happens when we actively engage in becoming a better human being — not perfect, but striving for better. To have others respect us, we must first respect others. And respect is not a one-time event. It is earned, not once, but on a continual basis each day throughout the day. How we manage life, both its adversities and successes, determines the respect we will receive. Give it, and you will receive it. Earn it, and it will be given to you.

K. Self-Discipline: Many of us drop the ball on this skill way too often; we shouldn't. It is such a vital part of success. Telling oneself to "Do It Now" works for us better than anything we've heard of or read. It's not a question of not knowing that we shouldn't put off until tomorrow what we should do today, it's the act of doing it today. Just do it; do it now. No guilt or remorse later. Besides, it's a feel-good. It's takes self discipline to do anything worthwhile. Listen to your own unspoken excuses and change the message to now, not later. Or whenever possible, delegate the task, but get it done instead of beating yourself up because, once again, you failed to do it.

L. Persistence: You'll need persistence to master the skills you need to succeed in rebuilding your confidence and becoming a person of significance. Persistence is a skill all successful people have had to master, and no one will achieve their goals and ambitions without it. It is no different than learning to ride a bicycle. Keep trying until it begins to work, and keep working it until it becomes a part of your being. When you fell off your bike learning to ride it, you got back up and tried it again. Remind yourself that life is no different today. Get back up, dust off, make adjustments, gather your support team, listen to their wisdom and encouragement, believe it and get back on the road to success.

Now that you've gone through these skills to identify the ones you need to improve on and practice, a couple of things will happen. First, your confidence will begin to soar. You'll have no reason to be defensive. You'll know where to go to search for the missing skill if you fail to accomplish your goal.

No need to be perfect. Just be good at what you choose to do and do it skillfully. You can be open and honest with trusted support-team members. Your cup will be full with energy, passion and confidence. Your drain holes will be few. You now understand why it appears easy for others and hasn't for you. You can be confident that you can achieve your goals and aspirations now that you know the skills you need to succeed.

> ***Oh, Yes You Can! Action:*** *Shout it out loud –*
> *Oh, Yes I Can! Repeat it as often as necessary.*

C H A P T E R   E L E V E N

Significance

Significance is having meaning or being of importance. We know that confidence is achieved when others recognize us as valued human beings deserving of their support, inspiration and help. Whoever they may be, they are people of significance. They are meaningful in our lives and important to us, to our success in doing what we want to do or being who we want to become. They have given of themselves when they didn't have to, however small or profound the contribution.

Most likely, they were passing along to us what had been given to them. Being the recipient of their generosity and encouragement, we owe it to others to pass that good will on. We have received, and now it's time to give. All take with no give is not a respected or acceptable character trait. Your expression of gratitude to your support team is to become a valued supporter of others.

"A person can grow only as much as his horizon allows."
– John Powell

You will discover that extending the gift of support to others does wonders for your self-confidence. It's a vital part of sustaining your confidence and raising it to an even higher level.

How do you achieve significance? How do you make your contribution, however small it may appear, to the betterment of the lives of others?

The first step is to realize that you are not alone. There are far more people lacking confidence than there are who have it. Everywhere you go, in all that you do, you come into contact with people, young and old alike, in need of more confidence, more inspiration, encouragement, support, hope, the need to be recognized or just to know their existence has value. It doesn't matter how they are dressed, the car they drive or the house they live in. You can have a positive impact, make someone's day or life better, regardless of their status and whether they are rich or poor.

Where do you start when it's all so very new to you? You start by using your skills. The skill of observation is a critical skill to start with. Observe your surroundings. There are people everywhere in need of an act of kindness. You may find them while in line at the grocery store, in an elevator, at work, participating in a social function, practicing your faith or while spending time with family or friends.

Look for reasons, genuine reasons, to pay a compliment or share something you've observed about that person, their character, their attitude, or something they did that you admire. Let them know you noticed and respect them. Often sharing with others the things you'd like to hear yourself is all it takes. After you've commented, observe how they respond.

There are also opportunities all around us throughout the day in which we can gain significance. They may seem small, but they leave a lasting impression of goodwill and kindness. Open doors for people; give up a seat to the elderly, physically challenged, or those with small children. Allowing someone to move ahead of you in line — someone you've observed to be struggling, elderly, or in a rush — is a memorable and uplifting gift to many.

Then there are those occasions when your act of kindness, developing your significance, seems insignificant to you, but is seen as quite significant to others. Imagine being in the post office when someone is searching for a penny or a dime. They can't find one. You have one and give it to them. Or the kid in the grocery store doesn't have enough money for his candy bar, but you have a dollar and give it to the cashier. Or you're at the drive-in window picking up a hamburger for lunch and give the cashier $5 for the lunch of the driver behind you. Imagine the thrill each will have in sharing your act of kindness with their family and friends. Imagine how special they will feel recalling your generosity.

Seek out those who are where you have been. You have a wealth of information in this book that you can pass along to others. One of the best ways to learn something, to make it a habit and part of your being, is to teach it to someone else.

Oh, Yes You Can! Action: Pick a topic or a skill set you want or need to improve on and teach it to someone you know could benefit from it. When you hear someone say, "I can't do that," or you know they're struggling with something in their lives, pick something you've read and learned from this book to share with them. Two things happen. You enhanced your significance in their lives, and you reinforce your learning.

We've talked about the negative taking up space in your brain, negative input that needs to be pushed out and be replaced with the positive. We've talked about your cup and closing the drain holes by eliminating confidence robbers and negative influences in your life, allowing positive influences to keep your cup full. You've identified the gold nuggets filling your cup. You are beginning to surround yourself with confidence boosters, those who are a good influence. Now it's your turn to be a confidence booster. You can become one of the good influences that help keep another's cup full. You may become someone's gold nugget. You now have all you need to be that person.

Throughout our careers, we have spoken with and interviewed people from all walks of life about their lives and success. In each story told, we hear how one or more people said or did something that gave the successful person the inspiration and encouragement to do or be more. It's been a family member, a friend, a teacher or coach, and on occasion, even a total stranger who made a significant difference in their lives.

We've never heard that it was a material possession that inspired their success — only words of encouragement and deep-felt beliefs by a supportive person, telling them they had the ability to live in this world with significance and leave it a better place.

We must include this because we've met people who think that if they help another, pay a compliment, or do or say something to make someone else feel valued or special, it will diminish them (the giver) in some way — make them feel "less than." That's simply not true. Being generous elevates us. If you doubt this, try it, and see how it makes you feel. Kindness is one commodity we give that fills us with more the more we give away.

We've met others who think they should expect something in return for giving of themselves — they see it as a trade. If they're not guaranteed something of like kind, they don't want to play. That's an entitlement attitude. It simply won't work if you want to become confident and successful. You have to be better than that.

Don't confuse your goodwill, your compassion or generosity, with being used by others. Users are defined as constant takers with no give. They are a drain hole. Users expect others to help them keep their cup full, but do nothing to help fill another's cup. Again, it's the entitlement attitude, and you can spot them in a relatively short period of time. Significance is not about being someone's doormat.

And too, there will be people who just don't appreciate you or your acts of kindness. It may be the person at the post office, the grocery store or a new neighbor. If they don't take kindly to your generosity or accept you, it's about them and not you. That doesn't mean you stop giving, although it is right to respect their desire to be left to themselves. But you keep on giving to others, whether or not you are outwardly acknowledged. Remember, it's not about a trade. Your rewards will come from others when you least expect it.

There is no better way to be influential than to positively influence others. If you want to be noticed, notice others. If you want to be respected and valued, respect and value others. If you want good friends, be a good friend. If you want success in all that you attempt, be someone who helps others succeed, and others will want to help you succeed.

Now you will be counted among the givers of faith, hope and inspiration, all of which fulfill the purpose of life. The more you give, the more you will receive.

In closing, remember there are three basic human needs among all people: 1) to love and be loved, 2) to understand and be understood, and 3) to give and to receive. You now have the knowledge and skills to fill each of these needs, which will give you significance throughout your life and in the lives of those you meet, each day and every day.

> *"How often in life we complete a task that was beyond*
> *the capability of the person we were when we started it!"*
> – Robert Brault

Go forth in confidence and be a person of significance. You'll never turn back.

Resources

Additional Books by Authors include:

DeLores Pressley: *Believe in the Power of You*
                                Clean Out the Closets of Your Life
                                Advance Revelations to Modeling

Sue Mackey: *Women Navigating Adversity*
                                Living Well Working Smart
                                Kids Navigating Life
                                The Honey-Do Survival Guide

For speaker bookings, coaching, consulting or more information contact:

DeLores Pressley
DeLores Pressley Worldwide
P. O. Box 9049 • Canton, OH 44711
Phone: 330.649.9809
www.DeLoresPressley.com
DP@DeLoresPressley.com

Connect with DeLores online:

www.twitter.com/DeLoresPressley

www.linkedin.com/in/DeLoresPressley

www.youtube.com/DeLoresPressley

http://www.facebook.com/DeLoresPressleyfanpage

Sue Mackey

The Mackey Group, LLC

P.O. Box 1247 • Issaquah, WA 98027-1247

Phone: 425.391.8776

www.MackeyGroup.com

info@mackeygroup.com

CPSIA information can be obtained
at www.ICGtesting.com
Printed in the USA
FFOW04n1702140915
16777FF